TECHNIQUE MASTER

53 Warm-ups to Revolutionize Your Guitar Playing

The Missing Method
An imprint of
Tenterhook Books, LLC
Akron, Ohio

Christian J. Triola

Discover what you've been missing.

Copyright ©2018 Christian J. Triola, Amy Joy Triola
All Rights Reserved.

Except as permitted under the U.S. Copyright Act of 1976, no part of this publication may be reproduced, distributed, or transmitted, in whole or in part, in any form or by any means, or stored in any form of retrieval system, without prior written consent of the author.

For bulk sales and permissions inquiries, please contact the author at info@themissingmethod.com.

Cover and Book Design by Amy Joy, ©2018 Amy Joy

The Missing Method™ for Guitar is an imprint of Tenterhook Books, LLC. The Missing Method name and logos are property of Tenterhook Books, LLC.

First Edition 2018, Tenterhook Books, LLC. Akron, Ohio.

ISBN-13: 978-1953101013 (Paperback)

Table of Contents

About the Author i
   What is the Missing Method? i

Introduction 1
   How this Book Works 2
   Overview & Recommended Approach 2

Basic Techniques 3
   How to Hold the Pick 3
   Fret Hand Technique 4

Unit 1: Quarter Note Warm-Ups 6
   How to Play Warm-Up #1 6
   How to Play Warm-Up #2 8
   How to Play Warm-Up #3 10
   How to Play Warm-Up #4 12
   How to Play Warm-Up #5 14
   How to Play Warm-Up #6 15
   How to Play Warm-Up #7 16
   How to Play Warm-Up #8, #9, #10, and #11 17
   How to Play Warm-Up #12 21

Unit 2: Eighth Note Warm-Ups 21
   How to Play Sixteenth Note Warm-Ups 29

Unit 3: Sixteenth Note Warm-Ups 29

Unit 4: Warm-Ups in Groups of Six 38

Unit 5: Open Position Warm-Ups 48

Unit 6: 5th and 9th Position Warm-Ups 50

Unit 7: The Final Challenge 54

Appendix 57
   How to Tune Your Guitar 58
      Guitar Tuners and Other Tuning Resources 60
   How to Read Tablature 61
   The Elements of Reading Music 62
      The Staff 62
      Ledger Lines 63
      Understanding Time 63
      Eighth Notes 65
      Sixteenth Notes 65
   Keeping Time: How to Use Your Metronome 66
   Resources to Help You Take Your Playing Further . . . 68

About the Author

Christian Triola is a professional guitar teacher and author with over 20 years experience using a scaffolding approach to instruction. This involves providing supports as students gain skills, then removing them as mastery develops. Christian has taught thousands of students in a way that enables them to learn and play music they love. He holds a Master's Degree in Education and a Bachelor's Degree in Music (Jazz Guitar) that help inform his student-centered approach. His books are designed to meet guitar learners' needs by filling gaps in existing methods. When he's not teaching, Christian enjoys writing fiction and hiking with his wife, Amy Joy.

What is the Missing Method?

We've helped thousands of students learn guitar through our step-by-step instructional materials. Our self-guided books for beginners explain guitar fundamentals in an easy-to-follow way. For building skills, we offer books on essential topics like note reading, scales, and chords, as well as a growing list of video courses and classes.

With our structured, skill-building approach, you'll become a better guitar player faster. Our materials provide ample practice so you can develop true mastery. Whether you're starting from scratch or looking to advance your skills, our books and courses will empower you to reach your guitar playing goals.

Learn more at TheMissingMethod.com.

Welcome to
The Missing Method for Guitar community!

We're dedicated to helping you master your instrument. To that end, there are a couple of resources we want to make sure you are aware of:

The Missing Method for Guitar YouTube channel.

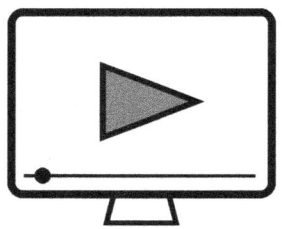

Here you'll find free weekly lessons we know you'll find useful as you work your way through this book, including tutorials on how to play your favorite songs. Find it at: https://bit.ly/Missing-Method-YouTube.

The Missing Method for Guitar Monthly Newsletter.

We only send out one a month, and you won't want to miss the updates on new resources, discount promotions, and more. Plus, when you sign up, we'll send you a free ebook full of exercises to help improve your playing. Sign up at https://themissingmethod.com/newsletter/.

Introduction

I once knew a really good classical guitar player who had to quit playing because he didn't pay close enough attention to his technique and ended up doing severe damage to his wrist.

I've also known players who claim they "can't play lead." The fact of the matter was they could have, if they would have developed better technical habits. The way they held their picks made it next to impossible for them to play a decent lead part. All they had to do was fix their technique.

Learning good technique, like anything that comes with learning an instrument, takes time. And as you can see from the above examples, not paying attention to it can be quite detrimental.

That said, you might be asking: what is good technique? Though there are specifics that have grown out of the classical guitar world, the basic idea is this: good technique sets your hands up for **maximum efficiency** while playing and **does no damage** to any part of your body.

Of course, I've also know players with less than ideal technique who still played well and did no damage to their hands or wrists. It worked for them. However, you'll still want to be careful and take time to develop your technique. The part that can be frustrating, especially for new players, is that good, efficient technique requires finger strength that a lot of newer players have not yet developed. The good news is that you hold in your hands a series of practice exercises that will help you develop your technique, both for the right and left hands, while developing your finger strength and timing.

> **Fun Quiz:** The player on the front cover is not practicing good technique. Can you tell what is wrong? (I'll reveal the answer on page 4.)

How this Book Works

This book is designed to incorporate focused warm-up exercises into your daily practice routine so that you can develop finger strength, dexterity, and timing in the most systematic and efficient way possible. It is divided up into several units. Each unit introduces a new set of warm-up exercises that get progressively more challenging. The last few chapters take you in a different direction, asking you to develop your technical skills while reviewing the natural notes from the open strings all the way to the thirteenth fret. Therefore, by completing these exercises, not only will you develop your technique and timing, you'll also expand your knowledge of the fretboard.

Overview & Recommended Approach

First, we'll go over basic technique for your fretting and strumming hands. Then we'll begin the exercises. These are written in both standard notation and tablature, and there are guides for reading each of these in the appendix.

Every one of the 53 warm-ups in this book are to be practiced with a metronome. Not sure how to do this? No problem. There is a guide for this in appendix as well. If you've never worked with a metronome before, you'll want to read through that before you begin. If you don't have a metronome, it's time to get one. Traditional metronomes are available at your local music store, and metronome apps are available online. Which one you choose is up to you. The key is that you get one and begin using it right away.

It is also important to practice playing with an in-tune guitar. Again, if you need help with this, a guide has been provided in the appendix.

The final warm-up in this book is a bonus 54th exercise. It is based on Warm-Up #1, but includes a new challenge for you to conquer.

Good luck, pay close attention to your technique, and don't forget to use your metronome!

Basic Techniques

How to hold the pick

1. First, curve the fingers of your picking hand inward, while keeping them relaxed. Don't make a fist.

2. Second, place the pick on top of the first knuckle, so that the point of the pick faces outward.

3. Third, place your thumb over the pick to hold it in place. This may feel awkward or uncomfortable at first, but once you get used to it, you'll have full control over the pick.

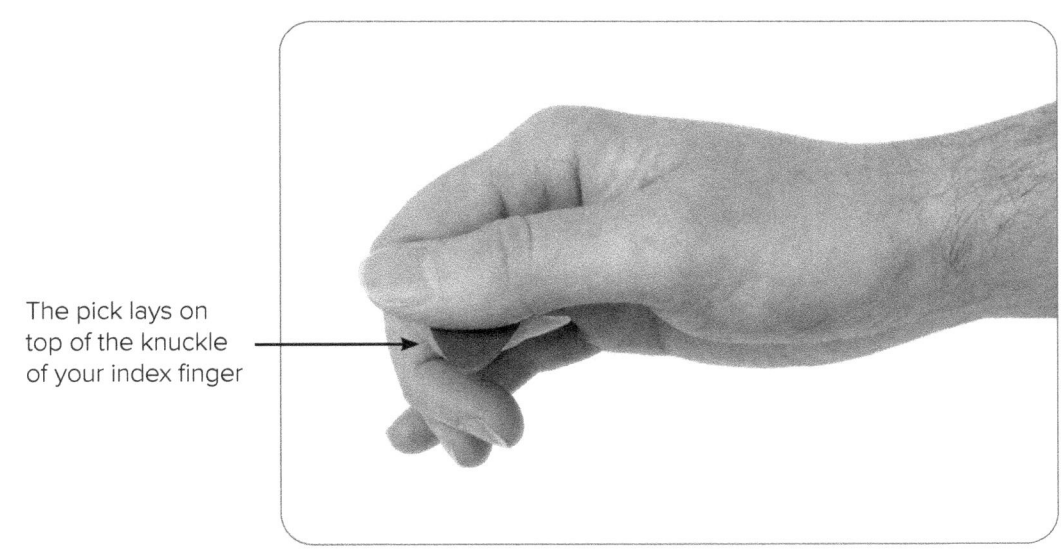

The pick lays on top of the knuckle of your index finger

Fret Hand Technique

Proper fret hand technique is crucial to getting a good sound and avoiding injury.

① First, always keep your fingers up on their tips. The fingers should be spread apart and not touching each other.

② Second, the wrist should be dropped down and the thumb planted behind the neck so that the thumb falls between the first and second fingers when looking at it from above.

③ Third, the knuckles of your hand should be running completely parallel to the neck, and the palm of your hand should not make contact with the neck.

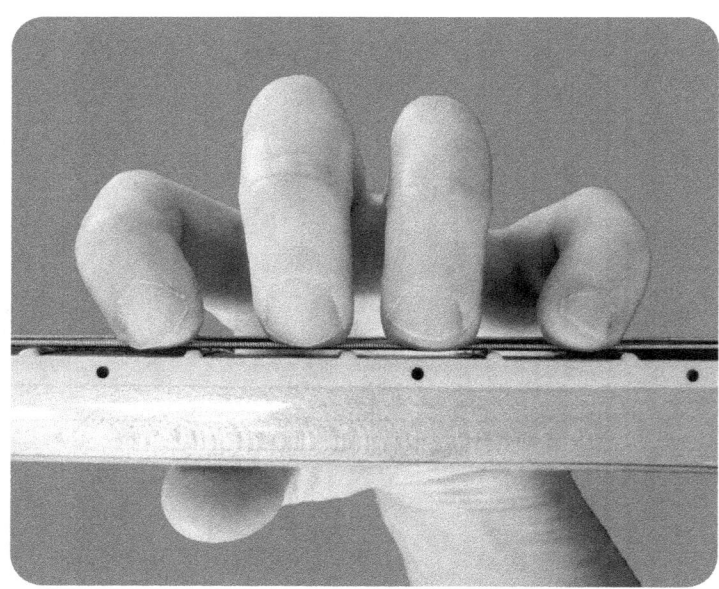

Page 1 Quiz Follow-up:

If you answered that the guitar player on the cover doesn't have his wrist dropped and his thumb behind the neck of the guitar, you answered correctly! While not every guitar player keeps to this practice, this is the most efficient way of playing, as it will help you reach notes while avoiding strain and injury.

Unit 1: Quarter Note Warm-Ups

How to Play Warm-Up #1

1. Before you begin, place all your fingers down on the last string (the thick one). Put your first finger on the fifth fret, your second finger on then sixth, and so on until you have all four fingers in place. Then check your technique. Each finger should be spaced evenly with your middle two fingers straight and the first and last fingers pointing inward toward the middle fingers. Make sure that only your thumb and fingertips are touching the guitar neck. Once your fingers are perfectly placed (see picture on page 4), then take off all your fingers but the first one. With your pick, pick down as indicated. When you go to play the second note, DO NOT remove your first finger, keep it down. Repeat this with the other fingers. Think of it this way: once a finger has been placed down, DO NOT remove it until you move on to the next string. Once you reach measure seven, this rule no longer applies. However, keep your fingers close to the frets.

2. Now that you know how to place your fingers correctly, your next step is to try out the whole exercise to get a feel for it. Take your time. It's easier than it looks. All you are doing is playing one fret at a time.

3. Once you understand the mechanics of the exercise, get your metronome out. Set it for a slow tempo, such as 40 or 50, relative to how much experience you've had with a metronome. Then tap your foot with the click of the metronome before you play a single note. Once you have the feel of the metronome, keep your foot tapping while you start to play the exercise. Play WITH the click, not AFTER. Anticipate when the next click is going to happen and play your note at the same time. This takes some practice and coordination, but once you master it, the rest of this book will be a lot easier.

4. When you get to the point where this speed feels too easy, increase the speed by 10 clicks on the metronome. Then play it again. After that, increase the speed again by 10, and again, and again, until you can no longer keep up with the clicks.

This first warm-up is the basis for many of the exercises found in this book. There should be no rush to move on to the next one until this one can be done comfortably at about 120 beats per minute on your metronome.

Warm-Up #1

(Continue picking in the same manner throughout the exercise)

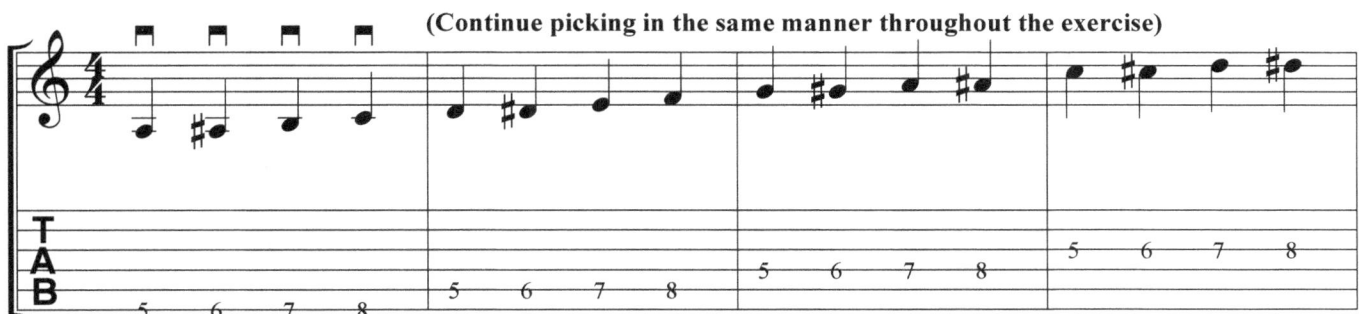

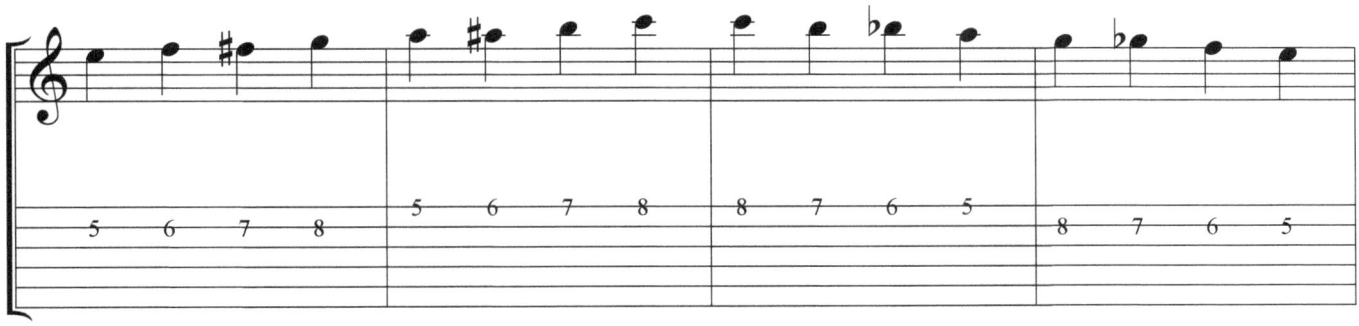

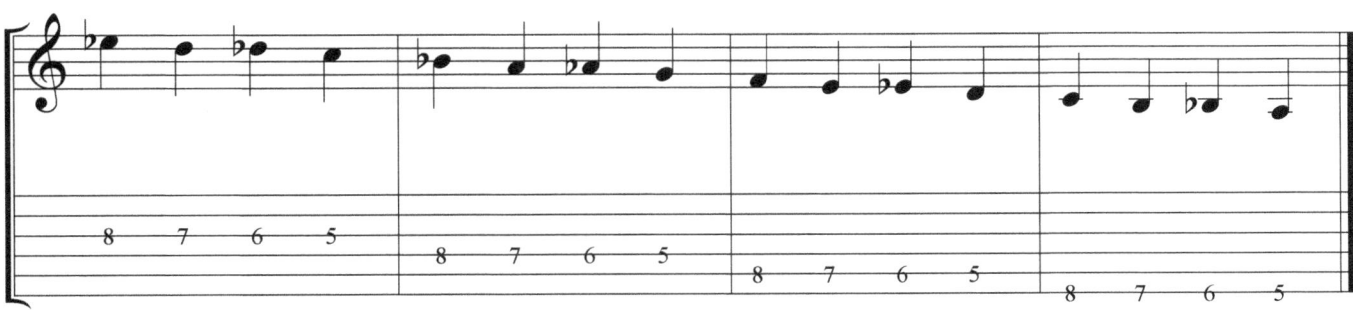

How to Play Warm-Up #2

Warm-up #2 is often called the spider walk, since that's what your hand looks like as you walk up and down the frets. To start this exercise, you'll want to position your hand the same way you did for Warm-Up #1. In fact, measure one of Warm-Up #2 is exactly the same as Warm-Up #1. However, you'll notice that things change right away in measure two. Instead of continuing on to the next string, you simply play a backwards version of measure one. You simply continue this for the remainder of the exercise as you switch from string to string.

Just like the previous exercise, you'll want to use a metronome. Again, start slowly, as slowly as you need to. If 40 beats per minute is too fast, there is nothing wrong with dropping it back further. That said, since you've conquered Warm-Up #1 by this point, learning this exercise should be much easier to do. Remember to focus on your finger placement, and pick downward and evenly along with the click of the metronome. Every note gets one click.

Warm-Up #2

How to Play Warm-Up #3

Warm-Up #3 is another variation on the first warm-up, but this time instead of playing the notes in order, we start to skip around a little. So in the first measure, for example, you start by playing the fifth fret, but then the second note is on the seventh fret. You'll want to read either the TAB or notation carefully in order to make sure you're playing the pattern correctly.

Once again, start this exercise with your hand in place, your wrist dropped, and your fingers ready. Then begin slowly, minimizing your movements as you play. Also, be sure to use a metronome. You'll want to start at about 50 beats per minute and slowly work up to somewhere around 100 to 120 beats per minute. Remember, you're working on precision and accuracy.

Warm-Up #3

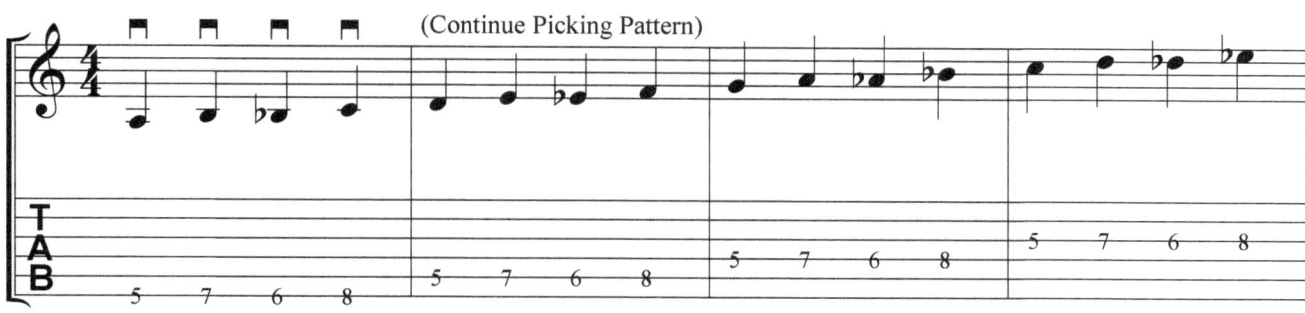
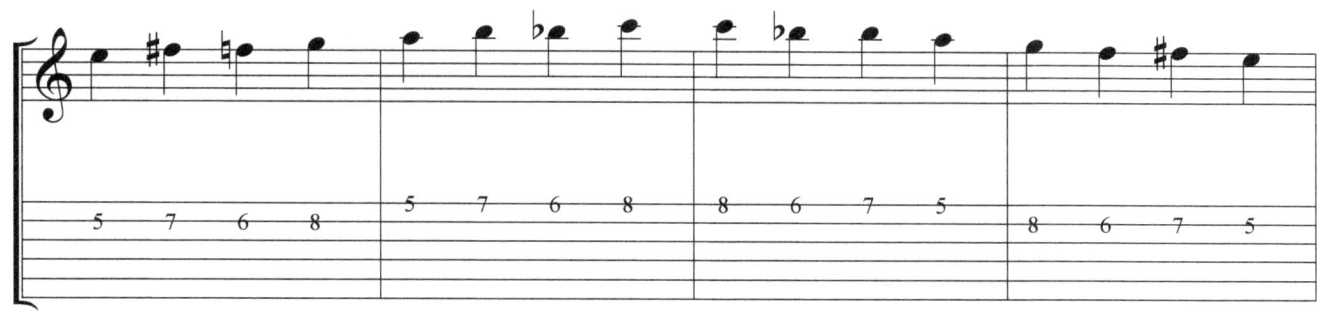
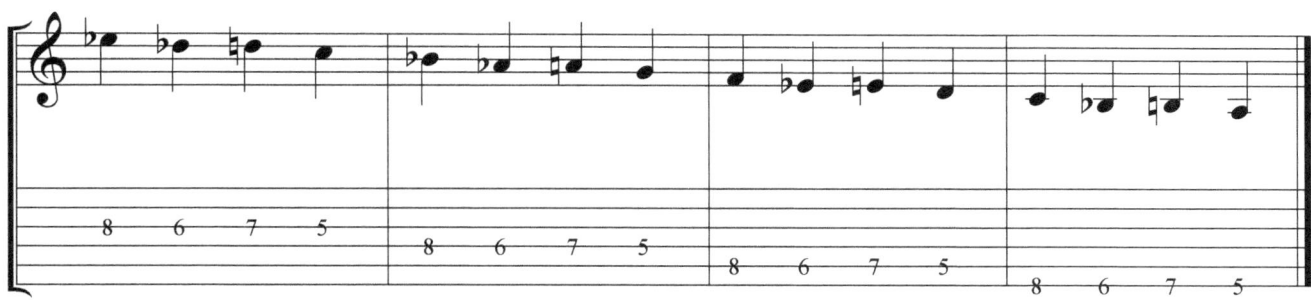

How to Play Warm-Up #4

This warm-up continues to mix up what you learned in Warm-Up #1. Notice that the time signature has changed to 6/4 time. This means that you now have six beats per measure. As always, put your hand down into position so that each finger is assigned its own fret. (First finger on the fifth fret, second finger on the sixth fret, etc.) Drop your wrist, and remember that only your thumb and fingertips should be on the guitar neck. For this pattern, start with the index finger, then play the note under the pinky. Then play the middle finger, and then the pinky. Then the ring finger and pinky.

Again, use a metronome in the same manner as you have with the previous exercises. Take your time, and slowly increase your speed.

Warm-Up #4

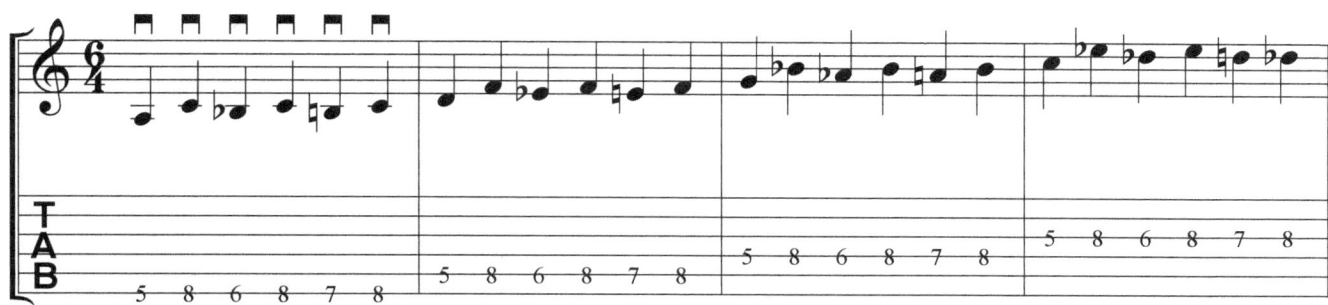
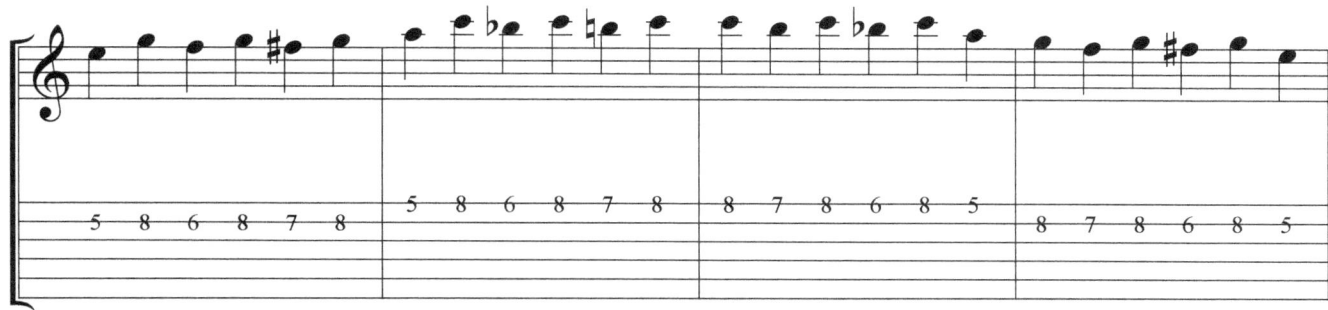

How to Play Warm-Up #5

Warm-up #5 takes the idea of working on one finger per fret in a slightly different direction. Instead of playing notes on one string before moving on, you'll only play one note per string, crossing over the fretboard.

Like the other warm-ups, this one follows a predictable pattern to make it easy to remember. Try it out slowly and without a metronome on your first attempt. You'll want to get the hang of it before you sync up with your metronome.

One more thing: be sure to pick downward throughout the exercise.

Warm-Up #5

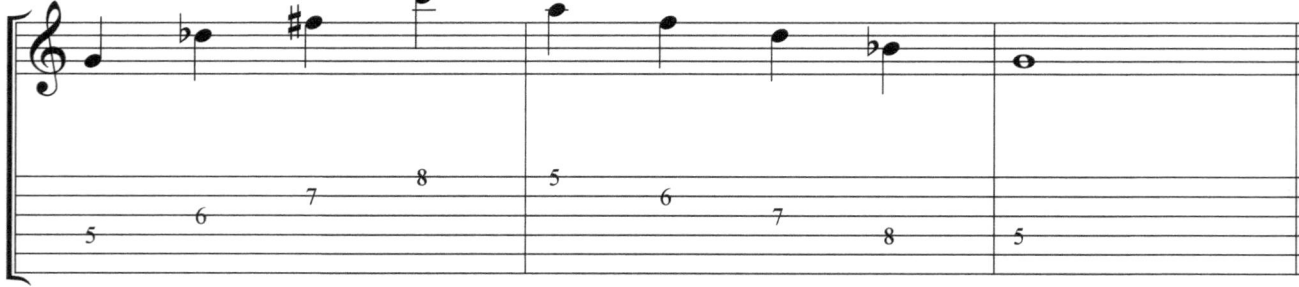

How to Play Warm-Up #6

This warm-up only uses two fingers: fingers 1 and 2 throughout the entire exercise. Even though this is the case, you'll still want to prepare your hand as if you were going to play Warm-Up #1. The goal here is to keep your fingers close by and use as little motion as possible as you progress through the exercise.

As always, be sure to start off slowly and use a metronome to help you build speed and accuracy.

Warm-Up #6

How to Play Warm-Up #7

This one is fun and fairly easy. You get to use your two strongest fingers to progress over the fretboard. However, just because it is easier to play doesn't mean you should neglect your metronome. Treat this one like any other warm-up: take your time, build speed, etc.

Warm-Up #7

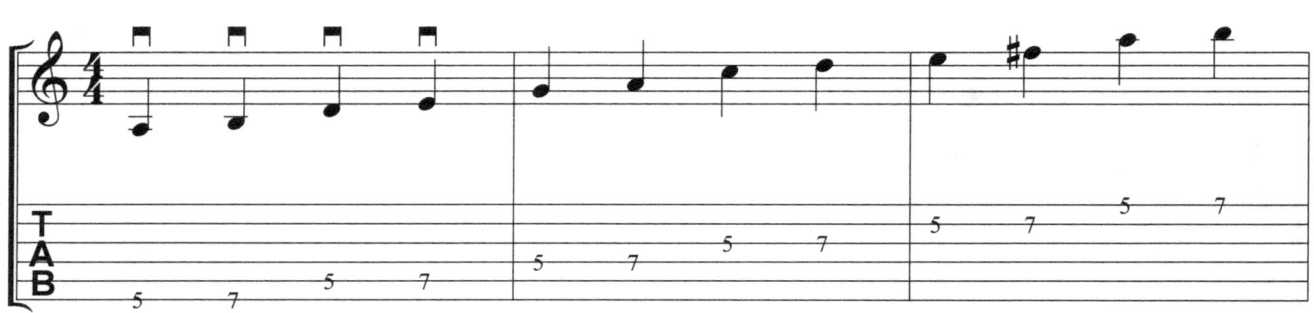

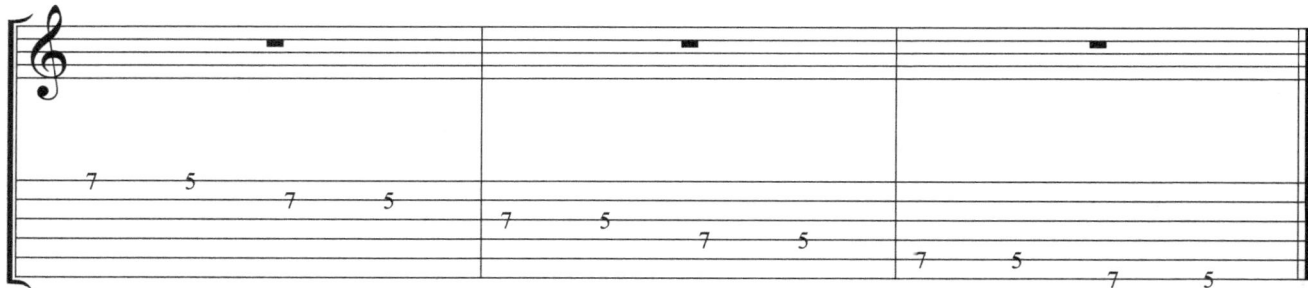

How to Play Warm-Up #8, #9, #10, and #11

The next several warm-ups all continue to mix up the different fingers into different patterns. Continue to only pick downward, use a metronome and build speed. These warm-ups along with Warm-ups #6 and #7 can all be combined into one continuous warm-up. So once you've tried them all and built speed, try to do them all back-to-back-to-back.

Warm-Up #8

17

Warm-Up #9

Warm-Up #10

A note on Warm-Up #11: since the pinky is often the weakest finger, this exercise my prove difficult at first, but with practice this can be overcome. So if you find it difficult, be patient and keep working on it until it is just as easy as the previous exercises.

Warm-Up #11

Unit 2: Eighth Note Warm-Ups

How to Play Warm-Up #12

In the last chapter, everything was picked downward, which is usually the case when playing quarter notes. In this chapter, we will be alternating our pick to accommodate for the eighth notes. Therefore, with each exercise, you will be playing down on the first half of the beat and up on the second half. That way, you will be doing more than getting your right hand technique warmed up, you'll also be working on coordination in your picking hand.

When using the metronome with eighth notes, be sure to tap your foot along with the click of the metronome. As your foot goes down, your pick should go down; as your foot comes up, your foot should come up with it.

When you hear the click of the metronome, that is your beat. The second half of the beat should be played exactly in between the clicks. This may take some getting used to, so be sure to try it out for a while before getting into the next several warm-ups. Once you think you've got it, set your metronome to 45-50 beats per minute and try it out with Warm-Up #12.

A note on Warm-Up #12: this warm-up is played in a similar manner to Warm-Up #1.

Also, note the down and up symbols in measure 1. Even though they are only shown in measure 1, you'll want to continue playing the rest of the exercise in the same manner.

Warm-Up #12

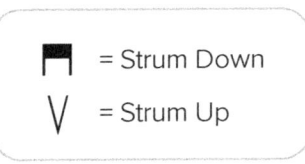

Note that Warm-Up #13 is the eighth note version of the spider walk exercise from Unit 1.

◫ = Strum Down
V = Strum Up

Warm-Up #13

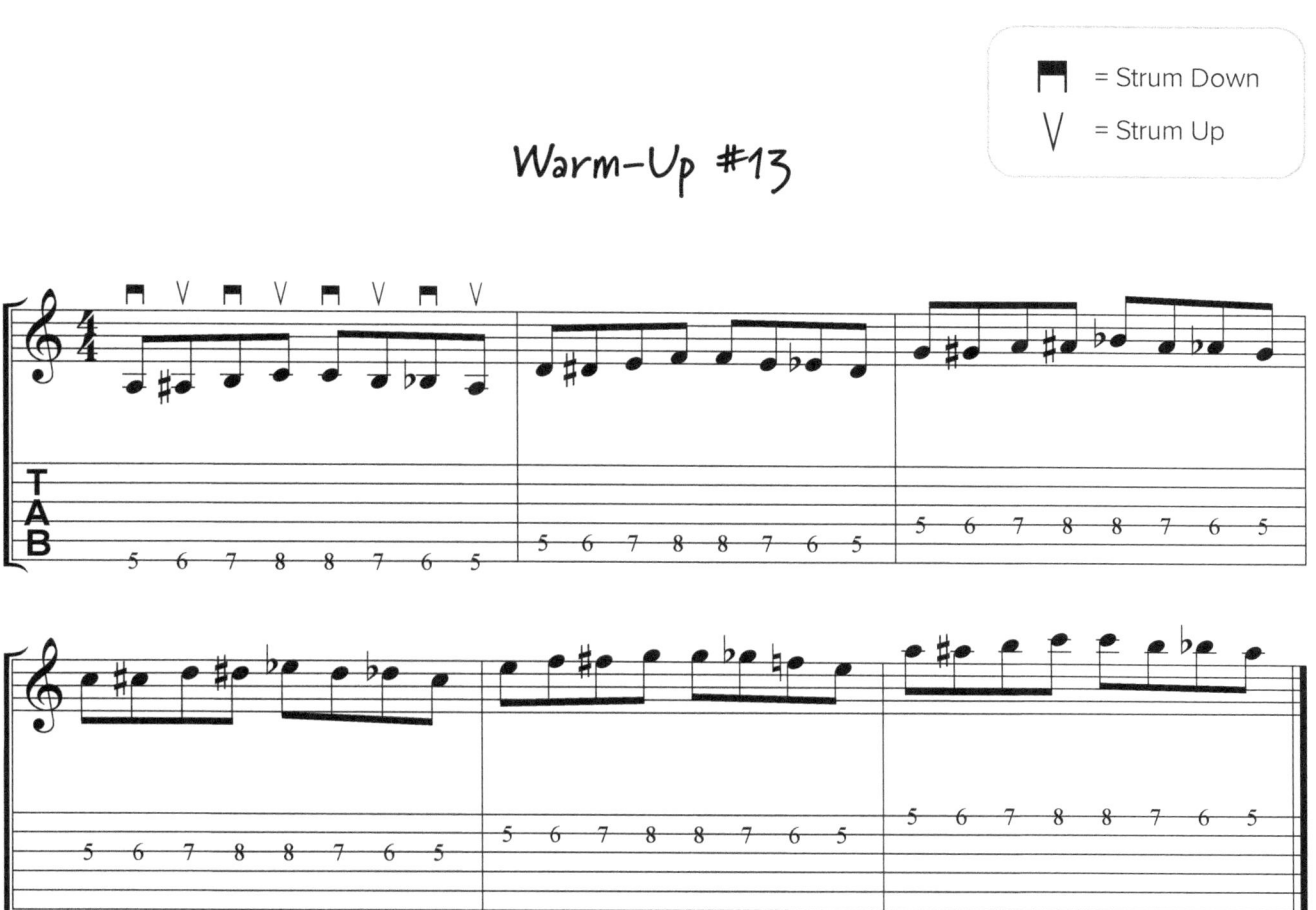

Warm-Up #14

Notice that Warm-Up #15 is in 3/4 time. This does not affect the picking hand. You will still need to alternate your pick as you play through the exercise.

Warm-Up #15

Warm-Up #16

The next several warm-ups use finger combinations in the same manner as their quarter note counterparts in Unit 1.

Warm-Up #17

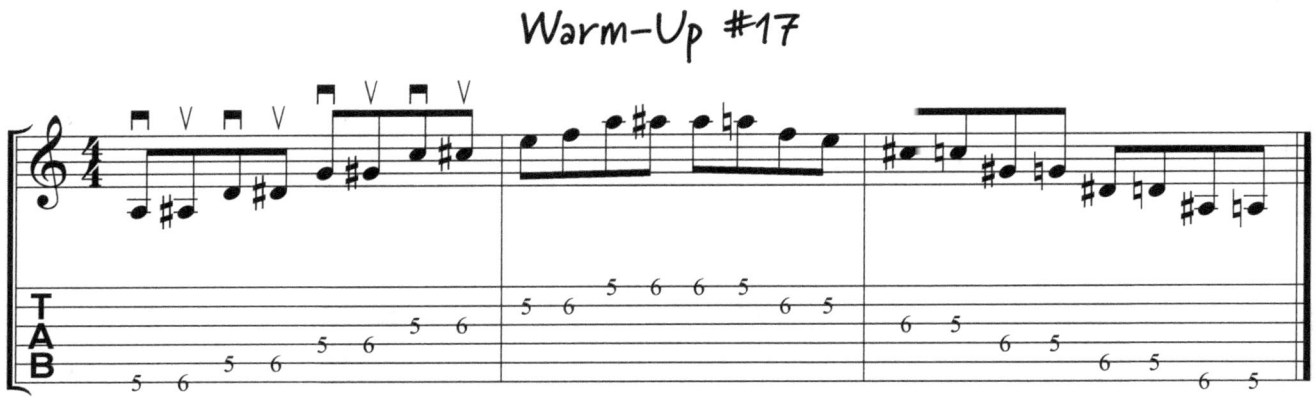

Warm-Up #18

Warm-Up #19

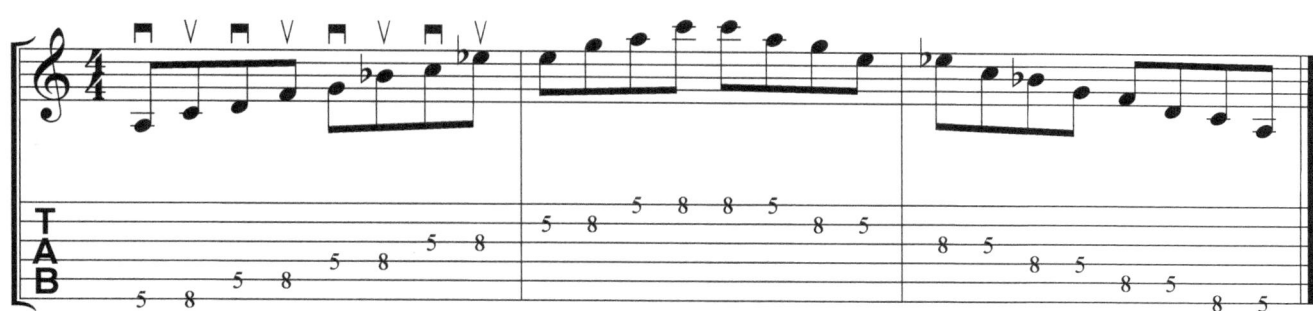

Warm-Up #20

Warm-Up #21

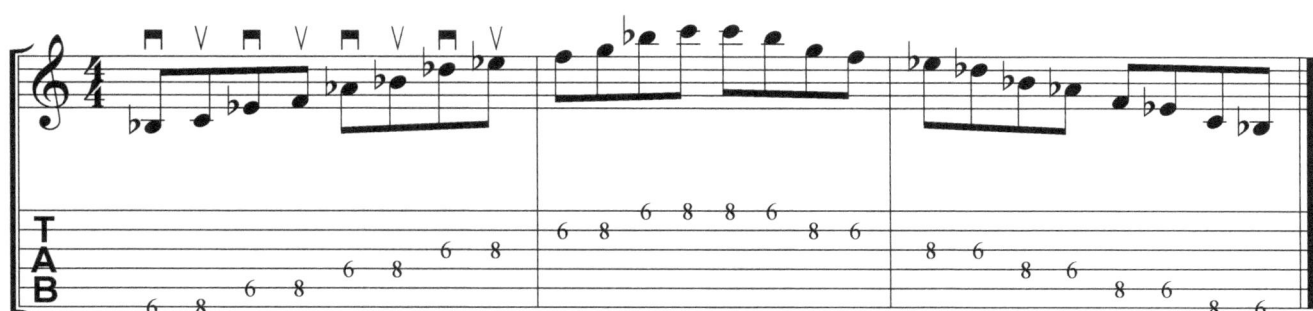

Warm-Up #22

Unit 3: Sixteenth Note Warm-Ups

How to Play Sixteenth Note Warm-Ups

Sixteenth notes divide the beat into four equal parts. That means that you play four even notes for each click of the metronome. Count: One Eee And Uh, etc. Since these notes are played so much faster, it is recommend that you work with just sixteenth notes before trying out the following exercises. This time when you tap your foot, play one note when your foot goes down, one more before your foot rises, another when it is up, and one last note just before it hits the ground again. It isn't as hard as it sounds. You can also think of sixteenth notes as four sets of tiny quarter note measures.

There are a lot of picking options for sixteenth notes, but the most common thing to do is alternate your picking. So in this case, you'll pick down on the beat, then up, down, up between beats.

Set your metronome at around 40 or slower if you've never played sixteenths before. If you have, I'd recommend starting around 50. And again, keep increasing the speed until you can't play it anymore. By doing so, you'll set for yourself a challenge to overcome. Most guitar players can eventually get their continuous sixteenth notes to around 120 to 130 beats per minute.

Warm-Up #23

Warm-Up #24

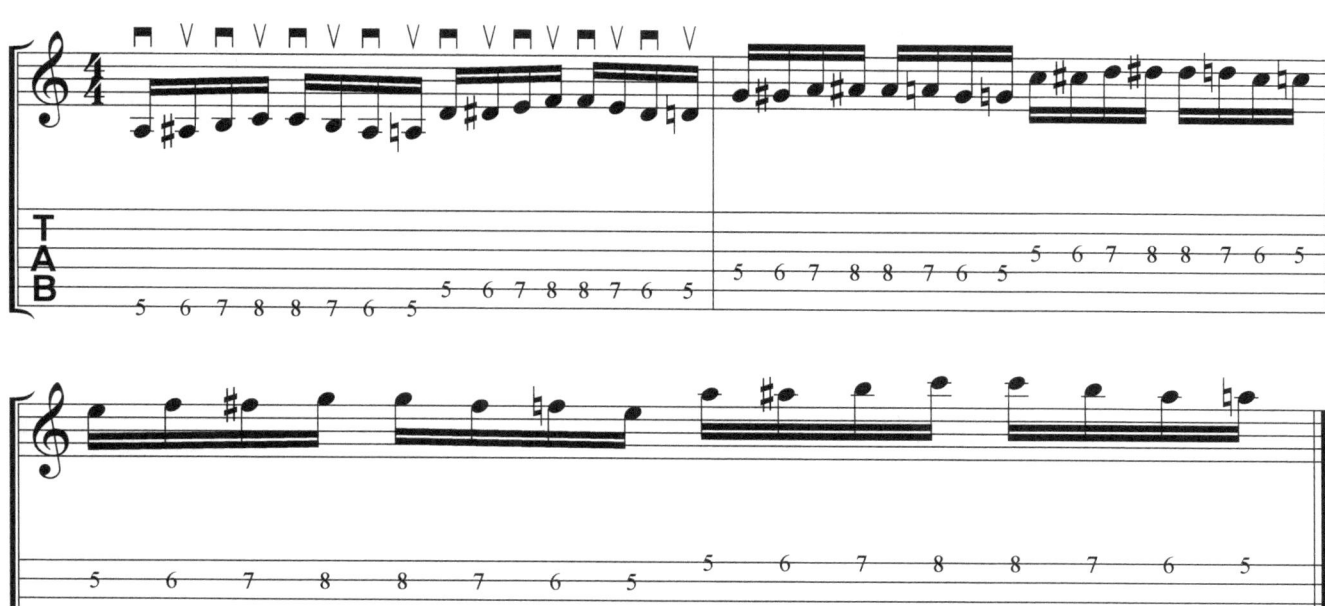

31

Warm-Up #25

Note that the time signature in Warm-Up #26 is 3/4 time. (For more information on 3/4 time, refer to the appendix, page 64.)

Warm-Up #26

Warm-Up #27

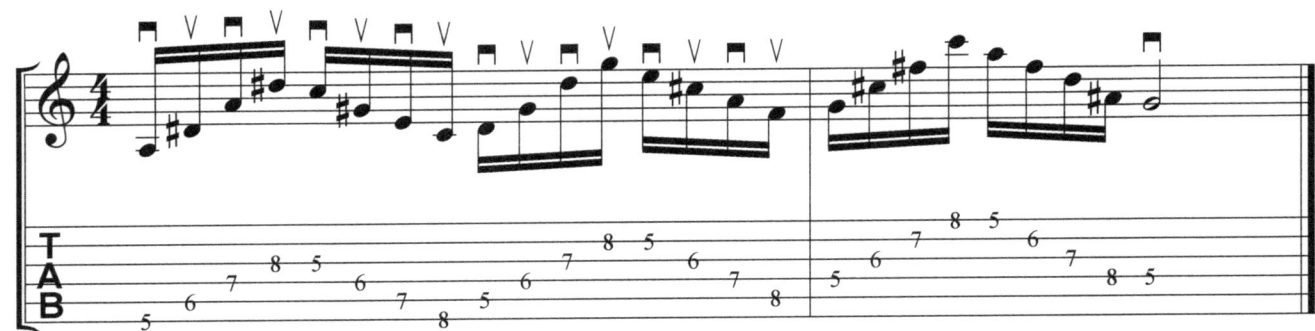

Warm-Up #28

Warm-Up #29

Warm-Up #30

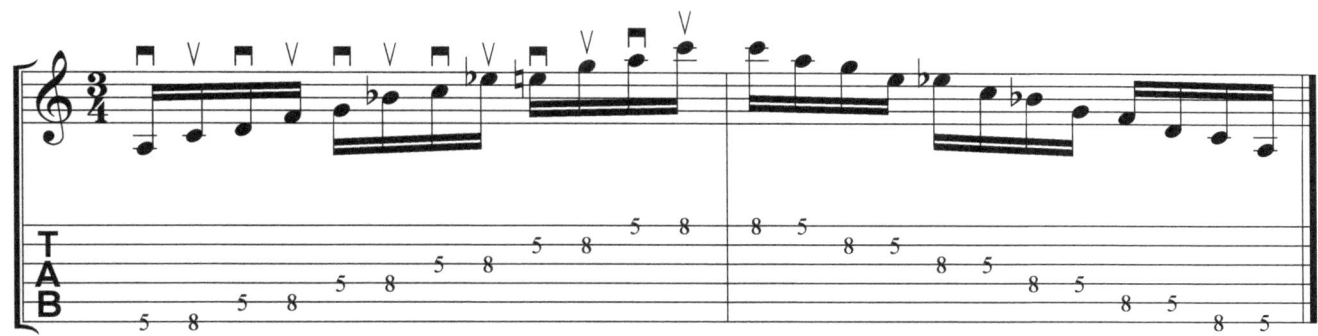

Warm-Up #31

Warm-Up #32

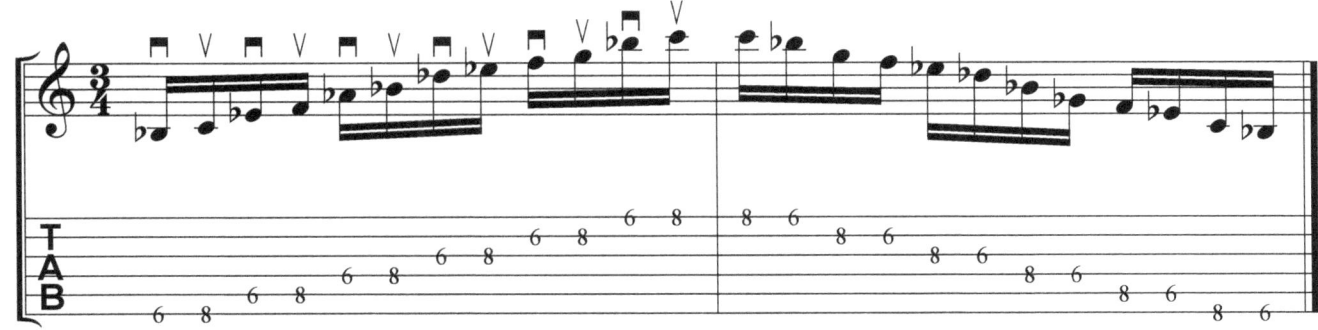

Warm-Up #33

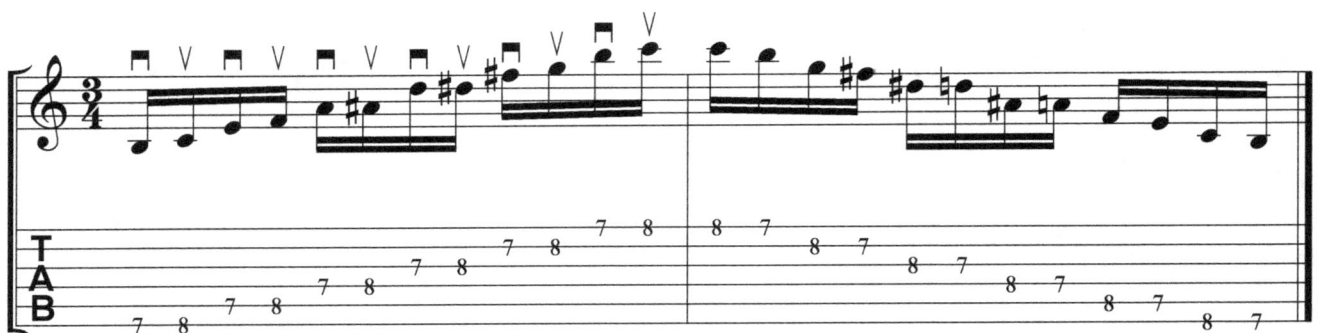

Warm-Ups #28-#33 Combined

Unit 4: Warm-Ups in Groups of Six

The warm-up exercises on the following pages are written in 6/8 time, which means there are six beats per measure and the eighth note is the beat. As such, 6/8 time also has what is known as a pulse on beats 1 and 4. That means that the pulse is represented by a dotted quarter note, which is three full beats in 6/8. Since this is the case, you'll want to set your metronome to just two slow clicks per measure, one for beat 1 and one for beat 4. So as you play through them, you'll hear a click on the one, and then another on four. Therefore, they are counted like this: One-and-two-and-three-and Four-and-five-and-six-and. Accent marks have been added to these exercises to show you where the pulse can be found.

Once you are able to play these exercises as written, to challenge yourself, think of each exercise as sets of sextuplets in 2/4 time. This means that the metronome will still click in the same spots, but it is counted differently. In this case, you would count One-two-three-four-five-six, Two-two-three-four-five-six. This is a great way to build speed and coordination. However, only attempt this once you've mastered the sixteenth note unit and the regular 6/8 exercises in this unit.

As usual, always check your technique before beginning. Keep your fingers on their tips and your wrist dropped. Only put as much pressure on each note as needed to get a clear sound.

Warm-Up #34

39

Warm-Up #35 is the 6/8 version of the spider walk. Here a new challenge is presented: since there are only four notes per string, you have to play two notes on the next string for each beat. Be sure to read through this carefully before you start the metronome.

Warm-Up #35

Warm-Up #36

Warm-Up #37

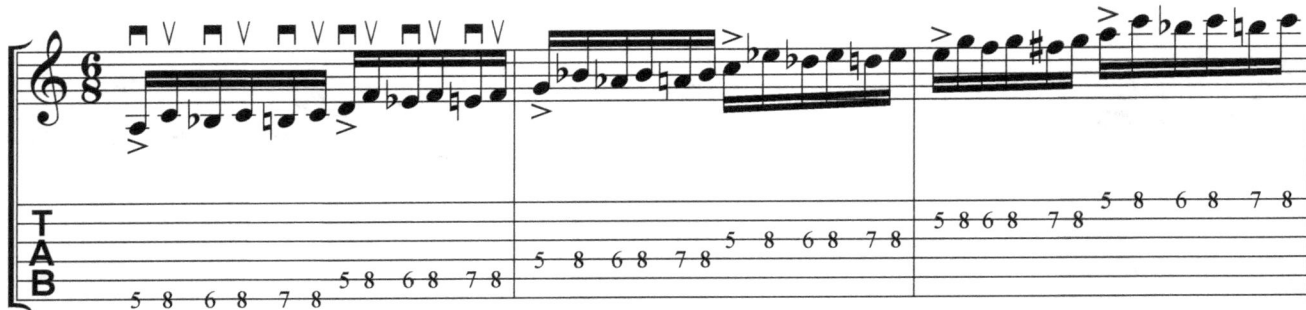

Warm-Up #38

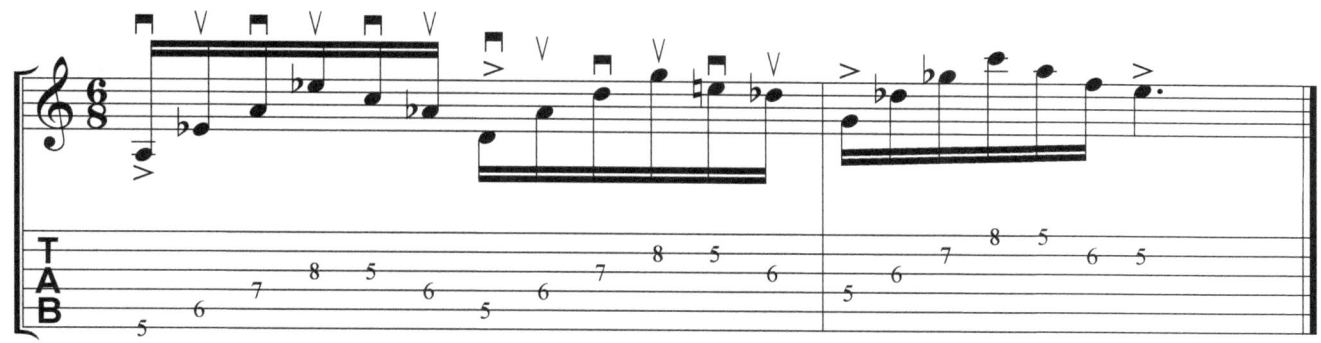

Warm-Up #39

Warm-Up #40

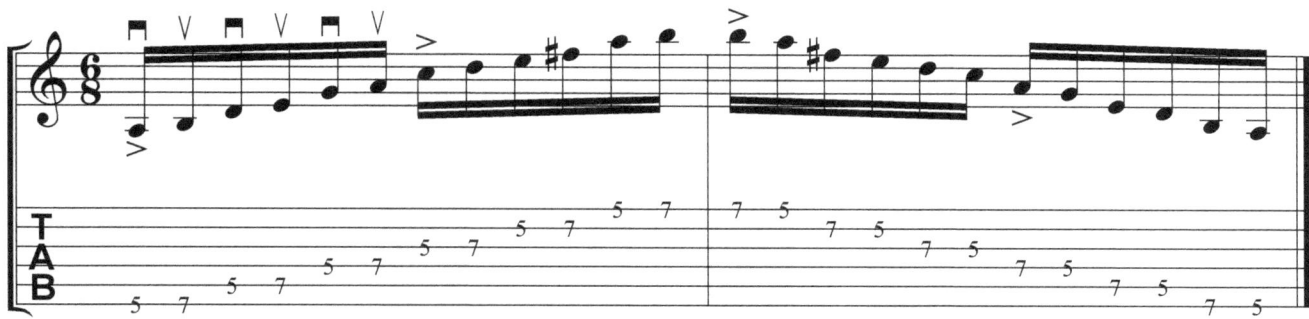

Warm-Up #41

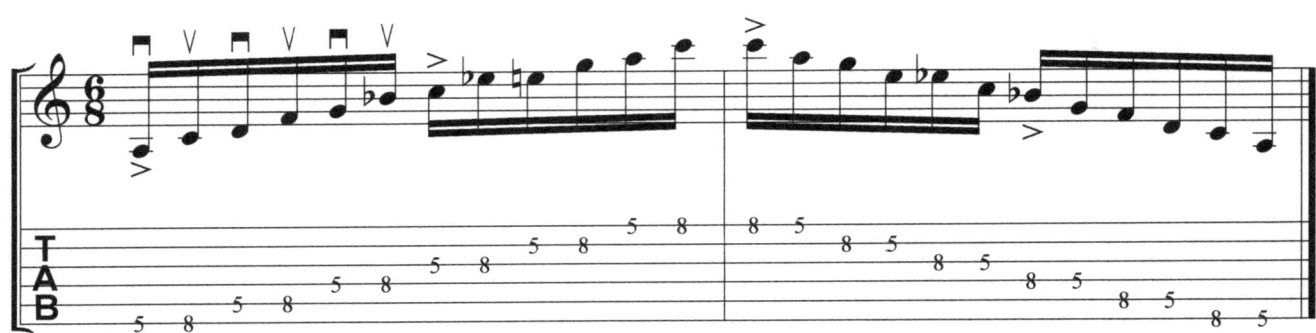

Warm-Up #42

Warm-Up #43

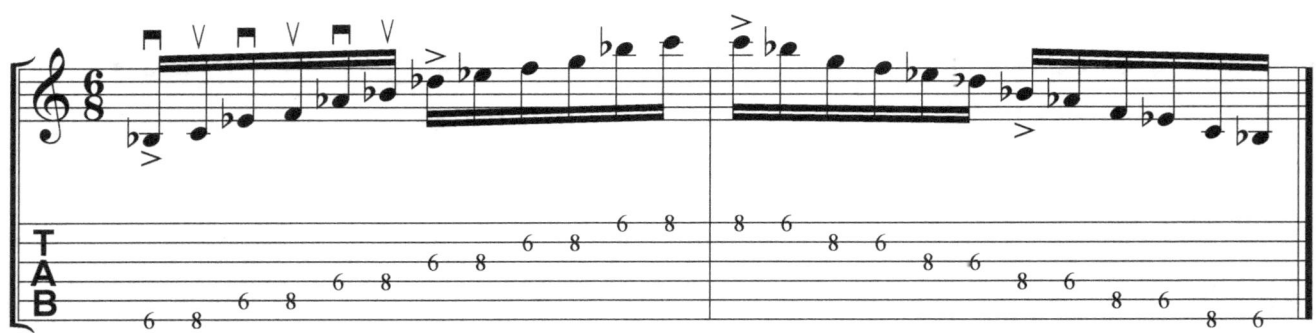

Warm-Up #44

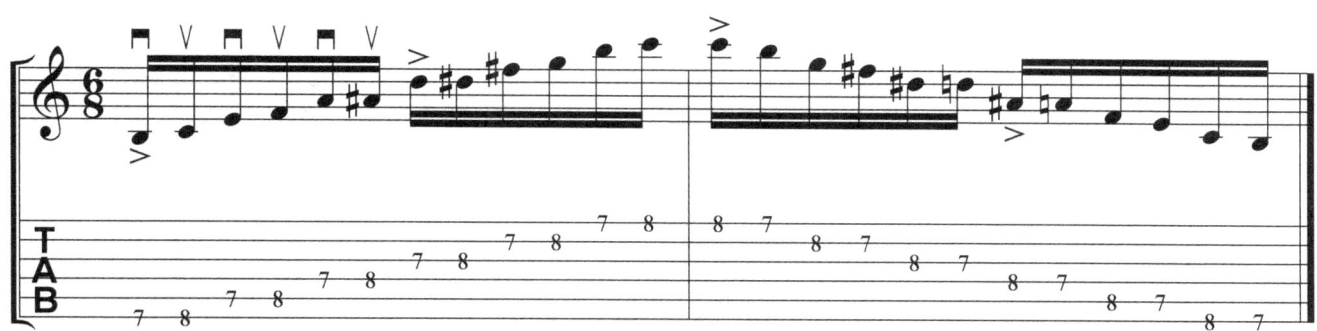

Warm-Ups #39-#44 Combined

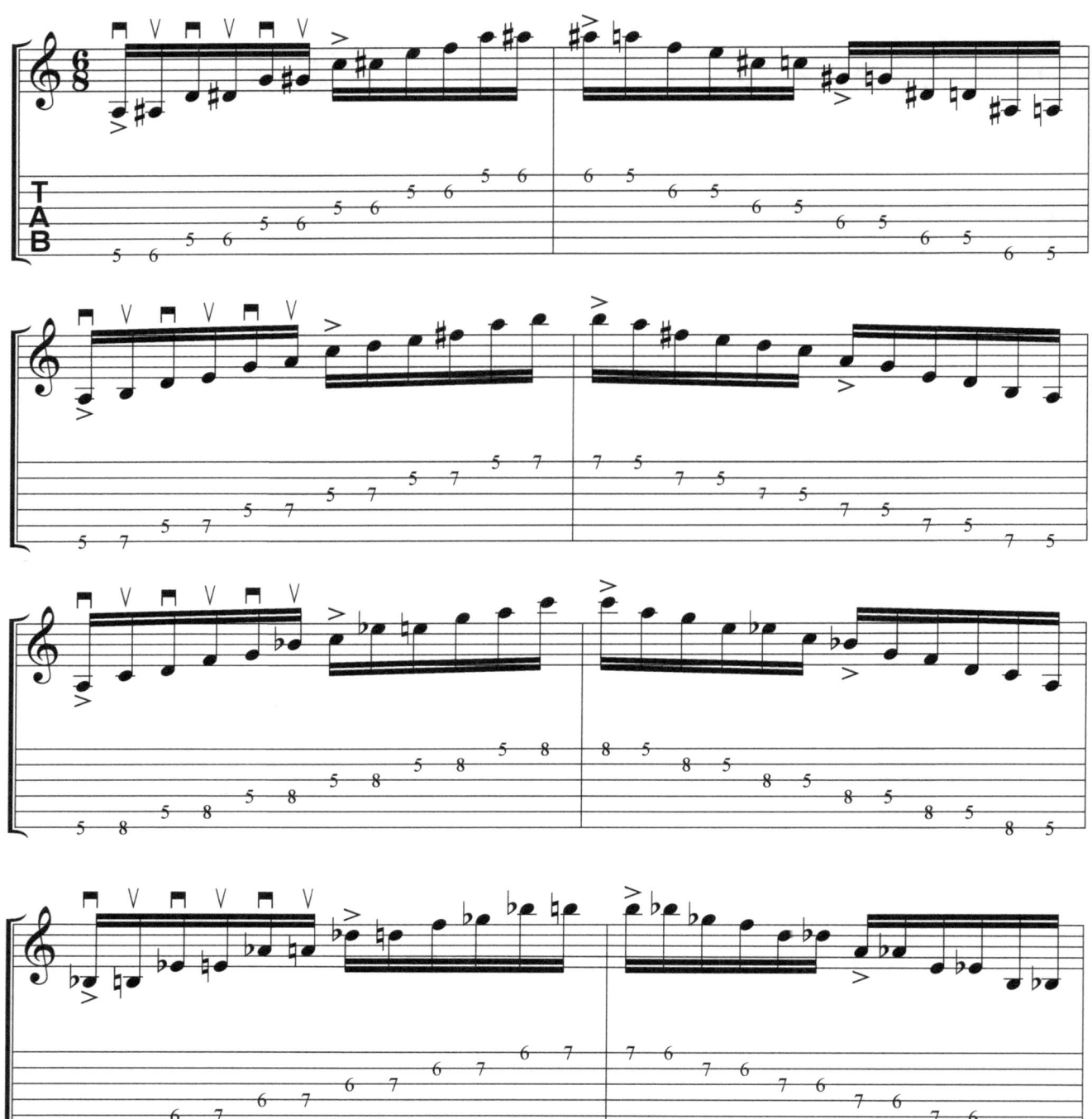

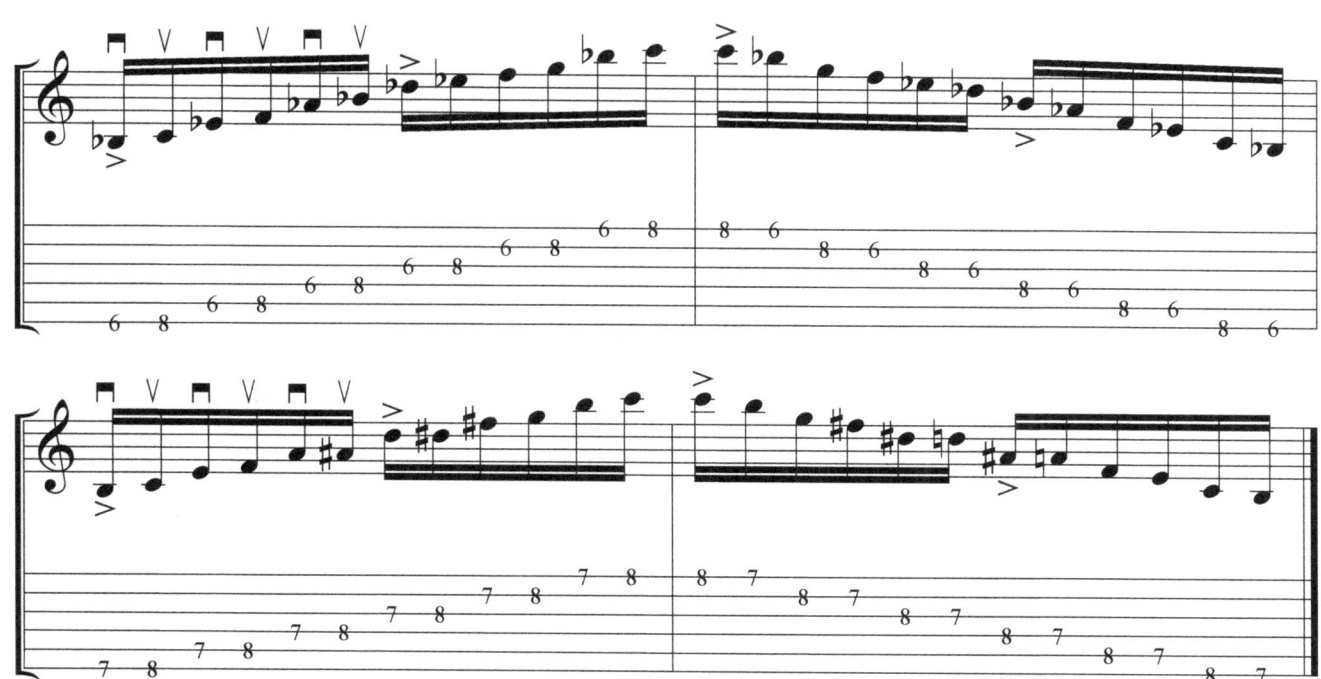

Unit 5: Open Position Warm-Ups

This next chapter moves away from the one note per fret model and starts to explore the natural notes on the neck (natural, of course, meaning no sharps or flats). Not only are these good exercises for technique, they can also help you become better acquainted with the notes on the neck.

To start off, we will be playing these exercises using quarter notes, then move on to eighths, and then sixteenths.

As before, always check your technique before starting, use a metronome, start slowly and build up speed. Play each exercise for one to three minutes continuously along with the metronome. That may not seem like much time, but you'll be surprised how many times you'll be able to play through the exercise.

Warm-Up #45

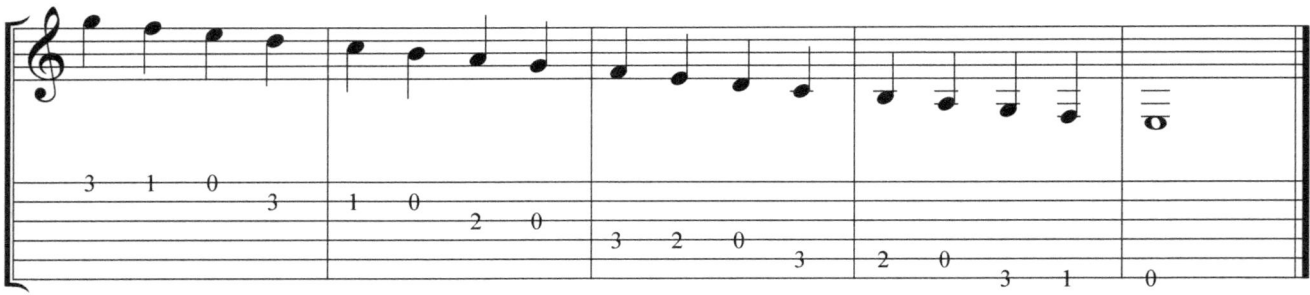

Warm-Up #46

Warm-Up #47

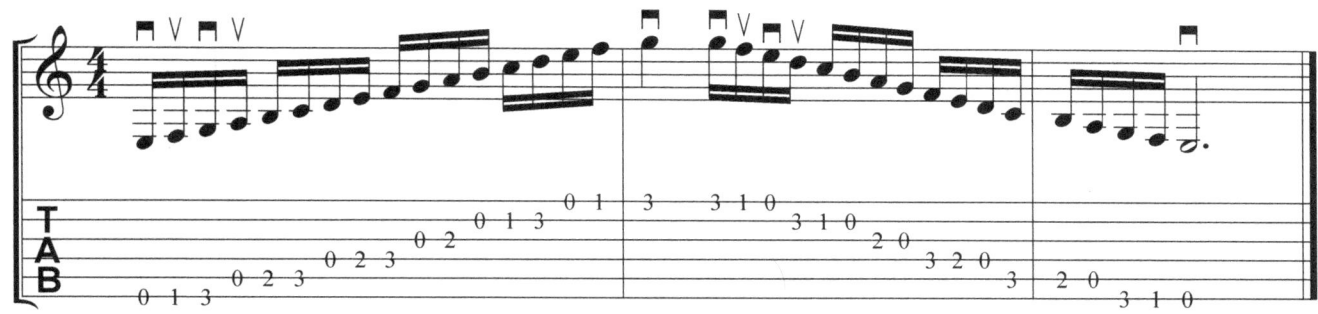

 For more on note reading in the open position, check out The Missing Method for Guitar Note Reading Series book 1.

Unit 6: 5th and 9th Position Warm-Ups

This unit continues to move up the neck as you practice all the natural notes from the fifth fret all the way up to the thirteenth. Once again, you'll start with quarter notes in each position before moving on to eighths and sixteenths.

Warm-Up #48

Warm-Up #49

Warm-Up #50

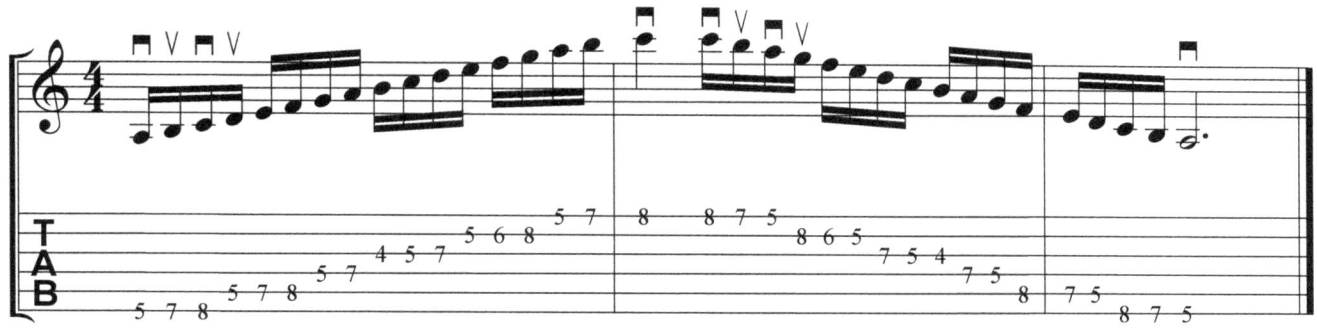

 For more on note reading in the 5th and 9th positions, check out The Missing Method for Guitar Note Reading Series books 2 & 3.

Warm-Up #51

Warm-Up #52

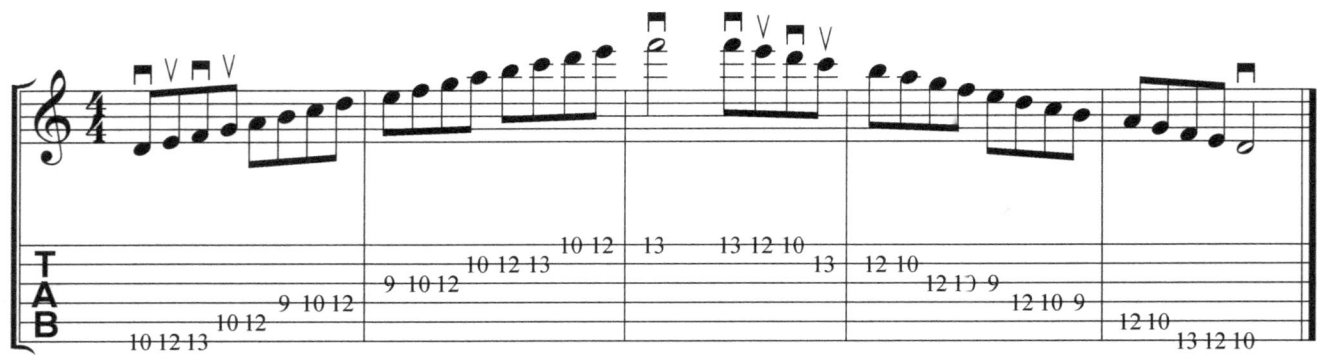

Warm-Up #53

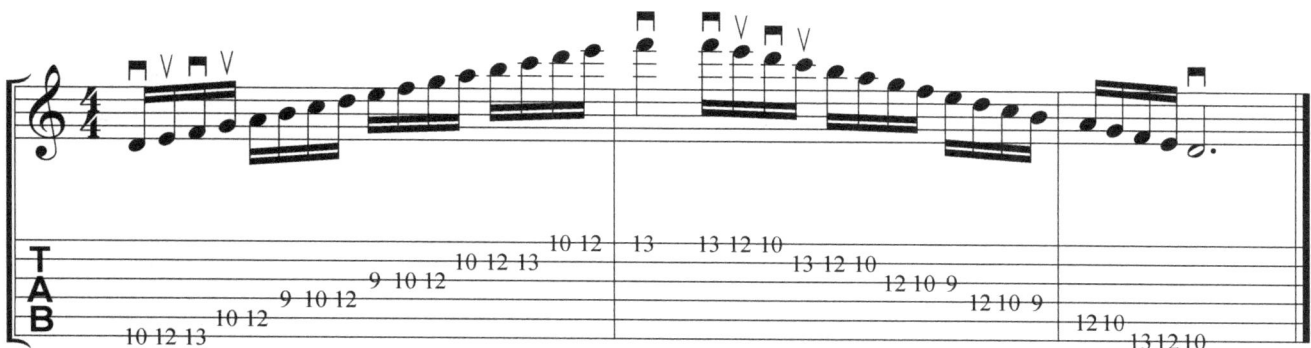

Unit 7: The Final Challenge

Exercise #54 should look familiar (since it is Warm-Up #1). However, this time we'll be adding a new level of difficulty. As you already know, you want to keep your fingers down as you move through the exercise so that by the time your pinky finger has played the final note on each string, all four fingers are still down on that string.

However, this time when you move to the next string, you should only move your index finger! Keep the other three down. Then, when you pick up the middle finger to move it, keep the first finger down, and keep fingers three and four down on the original string. That way you are only moving one finger at a time. Repeat this with the ring finger and then the pinky finger.

Continue in this manner as you move through the exercise.

Good luck!

Warm-Up #54

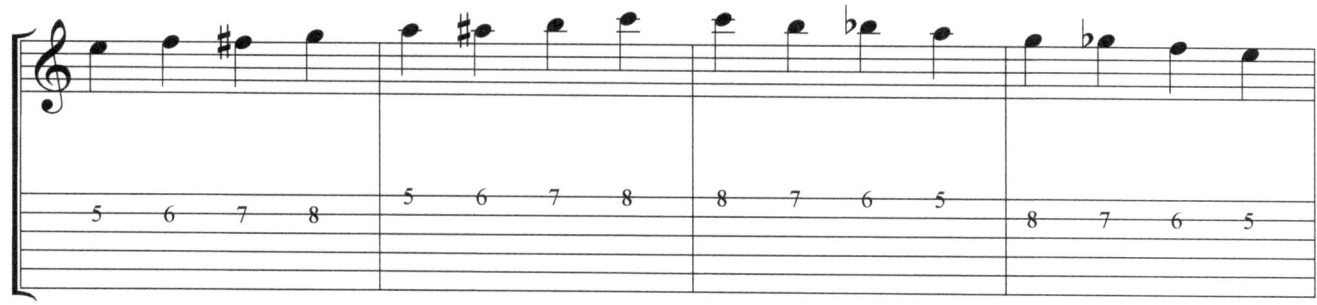

Appendix

- How to Tune Your Guitar
- Introduction to Tablature
- Introduction to Reading Guitar Music
- How to Use a Metronome

How to Tune Your Guitar

 The first thing you need to know in order to tune the guitar is what notes to tune to. The chart below shows the pitches of each string. Of course, if you are playing left-handed, these are reversed.

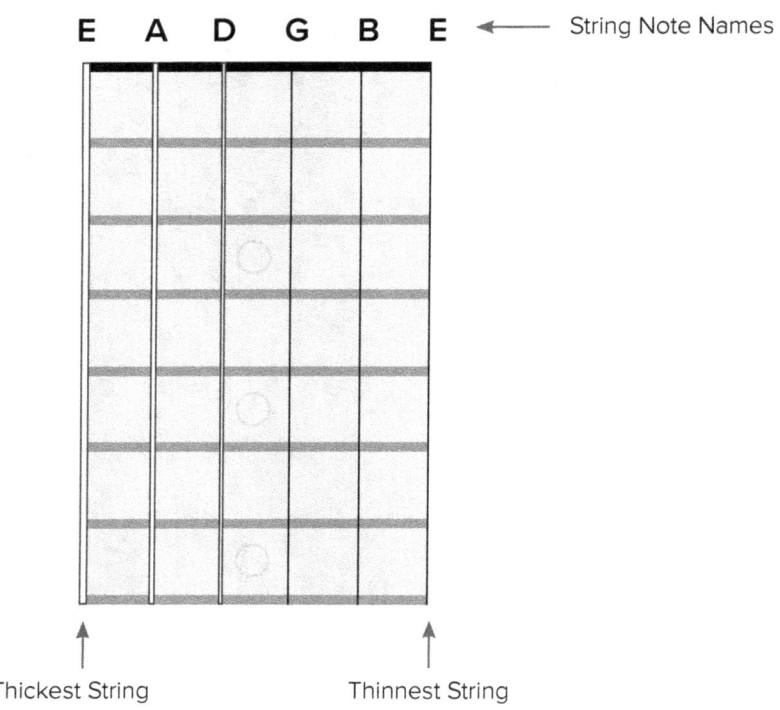

There are a couple of sayings that can help you remember the names of the strings, from thick to thin:

Eddie **A**te **D**ynamite, **G**ood **B**ye **E**ddie.

Or the less violent:

Every **A**mateur **D**oes **G**et **B**etter **E**ventually.

2 The second thing you should know is that tuning takes practice. It can be a little frustrating at first, but once you've done it a few times it gets easier and easier.

3 The third thing you need to know is that most of the time your guitar will only need slight adjustments. Once it's in tune, it will usually stay fairly close to in tune most of the time. However, it is recommended that you check your tuning every time you pick up the guitar. Be sure to listen carefully to the sound of an in-tune guitar so you become familiar with what it should sound like.

4 Now that you know this, we can begin tuning the guitar. There are several tuning methods. The best method is to buy a guitar tuner and learn how to use it. (You can find information on tuners on the next page.)

Typically, most tuners will show which note you are playing and then tell you whether or not the note is too low, too high, or in tune. Usually, a meter of some kind will display this information.

If the string is too low, you'll want to tighten the string, If the string is too high, you'll want to loosen it. Be sure to listen to the sound of the string as well. Your ear will help you figure out if you are going too far from the in-tune note.

Guitar Tuners and Other Tuning Resources

Tuners come in all shapes and sizes. There are credit card sized tuners, apps, and clip-on tuners that attach to your guitar. There are also good tuning apps available, and many of them are free.

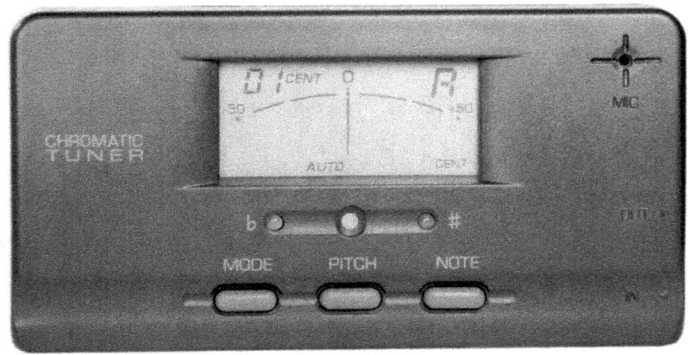

Another way you can tune the guitar is to use a reference pitch from an instrument that is already in tune. Most people use a piano, another in-tune guitar, or a pitch pipe to achieve this. In this case, you simply listen to the reference pitch and then match that pitch on your instrument. This can be difficult for beginners, but can help you to develop a strong ear as well as help you to develop your overall musicianship.

For more information on tuning, be sure to check out The Missing Method YouTube channel. There you will find video tutorials on how to tune your guitar as well as how to keep your guitar in tune.

Find it at: https://bit.ly/Missing-Method-YouTube

How to Read Tablature

Tablature (or TAB) is the most popular way of learning new songs. It is almost as old as standard notation for stringed instruments. The advantages of TAB are that it's easy to read and allows you to figure out songs much faster than standard notation. However, there are some drawbacks. Most TABS do not include any rhythm, meaning you have to either know how the song is supposed to sound ahead of time or rely on the standard notation, when available.

Tablature shows you *where* to play, while standard notation shows you *what* to play. Therefore, both are equally as valuable when learning a new song.

To read tablature, you should first know that each line represents a string on the guitar. The lowest string is the bottom line, and the highest string is the top line. (See below). Numbers are placed on the lines to show you which fret or frets to place your fingers. For example, if you see a number 1 on the first string (the top line), simply play the first fret on the first string.

The numbers on the lines represent the fret numbers.

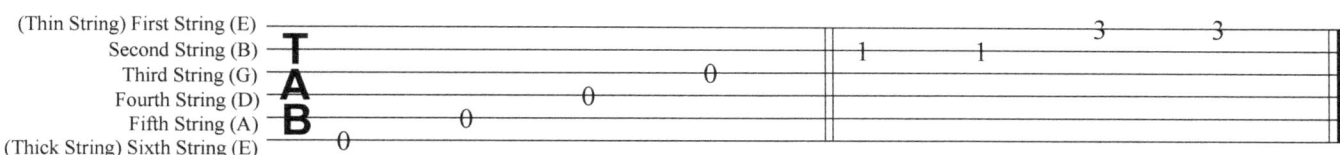

The Elements of Reading Music

The Staff

Long ago there was no universal system to keep track of what a song sounded like. For a very long time, the only way to have a record of a song or piece of music was to pass it on from musician to musician by ear. Eventually, someone decided to place a circle on a line and call it a specific pitch. After some time, more lines were included, and the modern staff was born. The **staff** is simply a chart showing the highness and lowness of pitches. The lower a dot (or notehead) is on the staff, the lower the sound and vice versa.

In order to know which range of pitches to perform, clefs were used. A **clef** is a symbol that tells what notes to expect on the staff. There are several clefs in music, but for guitar we only need to learn one: the **treble clef**. (Though it is recommended to learn bass clef as well in order to develop your overall musicianship.)

Staff with Treble Clef

The treble clef tells you what specific notes, or pitches, you can expect to find on its lines and spaces. The lines are (from low to high) E G B D F. The spaces are F A C E. Many elementary schools teach a pneumatic device to help you remember these note names: Every Good Boy Does Fine. And of course the spaces spell FACE.

Ledger Lines

It is possible to go higher and lower than what is on the clef. When this is done, the extra notes are placed on lines called **ledger lines.**

In music there are a total of 12 notes that can occur at different pitch levels. Each different sound is given a letter name. Thus the musical alphabet consists of A B C D E F G. However, this represents only seven of these notes; the remaining five notes fall in between these.

Understanding Time

The staff is divided up into sections called bars or measures. This is done to make the music easier to read and to help you figure out when to play the notes.

Each measure is only allowed a certain number of notes. This limitation allows us to keep track of time. The grouping of these notes is called meter. The most common meter is four beats per measure, or 4/4 time.

Beat is the underlying current of the music. You don't necessarily hear the beat. Think of it as a second hand on a clock, a constant steady clicking that helps you keep track of time.

What you actually play is *rhythm*. Rhythm tells you how long or how short a pitch should be held. For example, in 4/4 time a whole note is sustained for four beats. A half note is sustained for two beats. A quarter note (which takes up a quarter of a measure) is sustained for only one beat.

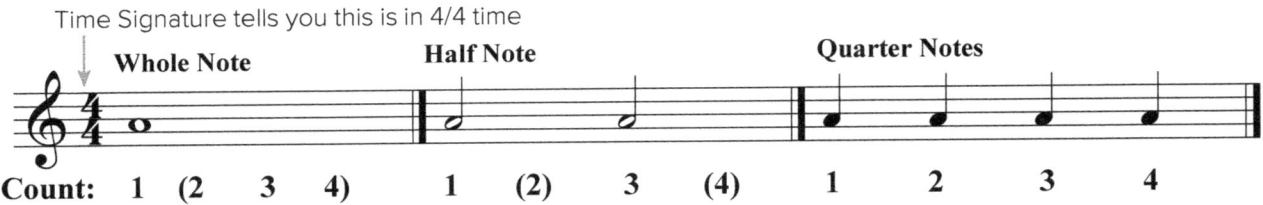

Besides 4/4 time, the second most common meter is 3/4. This means that there are only three beats per measure, instead of four, and the quarter note still represents the beat.

Eighth Notes

A quarter note can be further broken down into two eighth notes, each representing half a beat. When performing eighth notes, pick down on the downbeat, and up on the second half of each eighth note pair.

Sixteenth Notes

Eighth notes can be further broken down into four equal parts called sixteenth notes. That means that you can now play four notes for each beat. Just like eighth notes, sixteenth notes are often played using alternate picking. When counting sixteenth notes they are pronounced like this: One Eee And Uh, Two Eee and Uh, etc.

If you'd like to learn more about note reading, check out The Missing Method for Guitar Note Reading Series. With ample instruction and practice exercises, you'll master every note on the fretboard, in every key!

Keeping Time: How to Use Your Metronome

When you are first starting any instrument, practicing with a metronome can seem frustrating or even impossible at times. The fact of the matter is that it is something you'll want to get good at and *can* once you know how. One obstacle, however, can be physical movement. For some, it won't yet be possible to move fast enough to lock in with the metronome. But don't worry; with practice and time you'll be able to use the metronome without any trouble.

There are many different types of metronomes out there, from the traditional wind-up, piano top metronome, to apps for your phone or tablet. They all work well and do about the same thing. Their purpose to provide the beat for you.

Step One: Synchronize with the Metronome

To start using the metronome, turn it on and select a relatively slow beat. I recommend somewhere around 50 beats per minute (bpm). Before you do anything, listen to the beat. Then begin by tapping your foot along with the beat. Be sure to anticipate each beat and play with the metronome. Don't wait for the click then tap your foot. Tap in sync with it.

Once you feel in sync with the metronome, begin to count out loud along with the clicks: 1, 2, 3, 4, over and over again. Keep your foot tapping while you do this. Feel the pulse; feel your footfalls; feel the time, and lock in.

Stop the metronome, but keep tapping at the same rate of speed. After about 30 seconds, turn the metronome back on to see how close you've come. Chances are you will have either sped up or slowed down. That's normal. Everyone has a different heart rate, and this can affect your perception of time. But with practice, you'll start to feel different tempos and different meters.

Step Two: Practice with the Metronome

Once you feel comfortable with step one, pick up your guitar and take some time to get in sync with the metronome. To do this, choose any open string and play this string while you tap your foot, listen to the click, and count out loud.

Next, try it with any chord. Simply tap your foot with the metronome clicking while you strum.

After that, take any song or exercise and play only the first full phrase or measure; that way you can focus on the time more so than on the pitches. After one phrase or measure is complete, move on to the next one, repeating the process. Once you have a couple of phrases or measures down with the metronome, turn it off again and try playing just as accurately without it.

The key here is that you DON'T want to try and play an entire song with the metronome yet. Instead, use it to help you focus your practicing of small sections, so you can play them more accurately.

Keep in mind that even seasoned professionals still use metronomes to practice. It's the best way to help you focus on your timing, which is crucial for playing with others, as well as sounding your best overall. Time is often overlooked by new players since the early focus is on the right notes, chords, or just getting your fingers in the right spots. But once you have all that, you have to be aware of and practice your timing.

 Like tuners, metronomes can be found in a variety of shapes, sizes, and formats, including downloable apps.

Resources to Help You Take Your Playing Further

Pentatonic Master

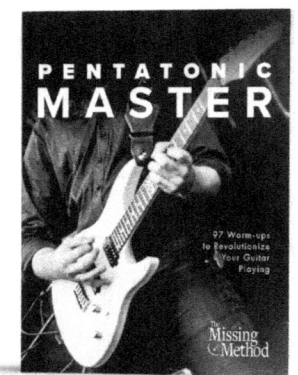

Every guitar player needs to know the pentatonic scale. It's as important to the guitar as learning chords, and countless numbers of songs and genres have used it as the basis for riffs, licks, and solos. Now, with *Pentatonic Master* you can master the scale all over the neck while you warm-up!

Major Scale Master

Learn to easily navigate the major scale anywhere on the fretboard. Increase your speed and accuracy, improve your timing, and understand the three-notes-per string approach, all while practicing the major scale in 5 different regions of the neck!

Perfect Practice

Rethink how you practice and get out of a practicing rut with *Perfect Practice*. Learn the secrets to transforming your practice time into time well-spent. This book will help you figure out how to identify and overcome obstacles in your way by showing you what to practice and how to structure your time to get results faster!

Guitar Chord Master™ Series

Guitar Chord Master is the only method book series that focuses exclusively on learning chords and strum patterns. Each book takes you step-by-step through the process of learning chords in a musical context, allowing you to master them for life! The series covers open chords, power chords, barre chords, how to use a capo, moveable shapes, and much more. Available in right and left-handed editions.

The Missing Method for Guitar Note Reading Series

Unlock your musicianship and gain a new level of expertise with The Missing Method for Guitar Note Reading series. You'll learn to read every note on the guitar, from the open strings to the 22nd fret. If you are looking to master the fretboard, this is the series for you! Available in right and left-handed editions.

Find these and more at TheMissingMethod.com.

www.ingramcontent.com/pod-product-compliance
Lightning Source LLC
Chambersburg PA
CBHW081755100526
44592CB00015B/2443